Makers and Destroyers
Glasgow Poems

What we have lost in our journey to here.

By the same author

Poetry available
Love's Troublesome Journey
The Belt Room
Scotland's Saint
The Sex Doctor
Curriculum for Excellence

Poetry coming soon
Wrong Ticket Home
Surveying the Wreckage
Janet: A Life in Verse

Biography coming soon
William Wallace (re-issue in Scots and English versions)
Robert the Bruce (re-issue in Scots and English versions)

Makers and
Destroyers
Glenn Telfer

Certain that someone out there likes this stuff.

Published by:
Big Ride
6/3 Pinkhill Park
Edinburgh EH12 7FA
Scotland
Copyright © Glenn Telfer 2013

Glenn Telfer has asserted his right under the Copyright, Designs and Patents Act 1988 to be identified as the author of this work.

A catalogue record for this book is available from the British Library.

ISBN: 978-1-909297-02-9

Cover by Glenn Telfer

Typeset by Raspberry Creative Type

Printed by Paramount Printers

Cover photo by Getty Images, Glasgow back court, 1956

Contents

Makers and Destroyers

wee shop

perfectly scaled to the ambitions
of a small and cheery child
and the small incomes
of the class of customer
your own wee shop

serving milk and rolls
to people you know
that are just like you
except for the wee shop
and the power you have

over the penny tray
to show a kindness,
Better take a hammer
to go wi that saw.
to a snottery toe-rag

that will be remembered
years after, as the small things
that reveal the big things,
like the essential nature
of the wee shop

the madness for growth
finds no understanding
Investment Returns? No,

this is just a wee shop
and a career

that is a gentle path
leading to a seat
at the bottom of your garden.
Success on a human scale
it works

no chance, on coppers
and brass from Lucky Bags
and broth mix of getting
too big for your boots.
Five Woodbine, Charlie.

A pint of milk, a plain loaf, and a wee pat of fresh
butter: 3/2d

The Language of Finn

I did not know then it was
the language of Finn
that reached back to
The Garden of Eden
and spoke of birds
and lochs and sky.
That it made honey
of words in a poem
or tears in a song.

We heard no singing
back from the pub
the door would bang
the scratch of chairs on
bare floorboards carried
through the silent night
then a voice beer loud
and another following it
turning up the volume
to a full scale bawling match
in an alien tongue.

Hearing it that first time in bed
I cooried into my granny's back
What is it Granny?
Och, they're fighting about toast.
One ate the others slice.
How do you know?

Oh, you can tell.
Go back to sleep, it'll be alright.
They're making more.

Playing out the back we
kept clear of their window.
Once, seeing them leave
we spied through a wee crack
where the cardboard covering
broken glass had peeled back.
The sticky rancid whiff of animals
rushed through the space

bare light bulb hardly a surprise
two broken chairs tied with string
fish supper wrappers beer bottles
cigarette ends box bed heaped
with filth coloured blankets
dirt clung to the random crockery
like a lichen

a broken crippled table
leaned on the mantle
above the ever unlit fire
(after cutting peat for free
never got used to paying for coal)
the cold was furious
it could have been a cage, except

for evidence of the finer things in life;
a tele and a picture of the Pope
tacked to the wall.
For support.

There were two of them
brothers, twins I think, big hulking
oxen made for navvying
coal scuttle hands
fiercely purple weather scoured
beer damaged faces.
In that place of wee men
they were a race apart

but docile, heads down avoiding
eyes, minimal nod of recognition
They're just two big, shy laddies.
Maybe, but not at midnight
after an evening getting tanked
at The Clachan.

All the bottled up misery
of their broken race…
let loose on each other
Leig as mi, you bastard!
as they roared and wrestled
punched and smashed
yet again their den and their faces.

In an age before house phones
for the likes of us
there was no-one to break it up
with a call to the police
far less a chap at the door,
*Lads, would you mind killing each other
a bit quieter?*

And then suddenly
after all the crashing
*B'fhear leum nach robh mi
riamh air a thighinn a sco!**
like two giant berserkers who
beating themselves senseless
simultaneously deliver the goodnight
blow to each other and fall
unconscious in a pile.
Total silence.

The journey from the croft
to Glasgow's golden paved streets
hadn't turned out like they'd hoped
swapping one hurting land for another
and the penny poverty of a single end
in that barren bothy of a home

hours ticked away to years
as they staggered towards

The Land of the Leal
8 pints at a time.
No wife to cook their dinner
How was work today, Dear?
Instead, a bitter marriage to each other
and another fish supper for tea.

A life given to the shovel and the drink
and waiting, waiting for the banshee's call
to take them to the croft
that's owned outright forever
beyond the landlord's reach.
Home at last, *Dhachaidh mu dheiridh thall.*

* *I wish I'd never came here!*

Makers and Destroyers: a Glasgow Diptych

Road builders

making a world with lolly sticks
sideways scraped in the dirt
no need for shops and houses
this is boys' world and
we only need roads
for our cars and lorries.

Footering about, getting things
lined up, making traffic lights
with wee stones and garages
from midden cans, everything
had to be perfect for me
that car sits next to the bus.

Impatient with my elaboration
you knocked off early
and were already chasing
baddies in a police car before
the roads were finished or
we had made our Highway Code.

Already in miniature the adults
we would become. I worry.
You do. Amazingly, we never
fought our alternative approaches
to road building complementary
our world big enough for two.

I lay out the cars carefully
and spent time thinking
about how petrol will be delivered
you get on with the business
of driving racing crashing.
Especially crashing.

Car thieves

A shadow appeared in our land
two big boys passing through
right away we knew what
they were about
bandits on a chevauchee
knew their being here

was due to us being alone
no-one hanging the washing
or big brothers nearby
our game stopped theirs started
a roughly spoken but polite
enough query, *Cnaseeyermota?*

said the way a leopard might
when considering its prey
a little voice inside my head
said, shout up for your granny.
Ma mammy sayd Ah'm no allowed.
Aye, bit she's no here the noo.

A brief stand-off, then the end-game
skilled by instinct following quickly
a classic ploy; the distraction
car crash caused by big feet
our emergency services rush to help
they bent down grabbed your racing car,

my red Mobil Oil tanker rushing
through the close to escape
fleeing on the road that they too
had built for themselves leading
in time to the gates
of the Big Hoose up the road.

Leaving us with a dubious distinction; five year old victims of car crime.

Stairheid Commando

Though you did not know it
this world, your world, was
an Escher painting made real.
Steps and stairs everywhere you turned
connecting small space to small space;
a hemmed-in world in 3D.

The first challenge; single steps.
Taken carefully, backwards
and on your knees
sliding out one leg, then the other,
in case you should tumble
who knows how far.

Eventually a wee run
could be faced without fear,
but still slowly
as the technique had yet to be mastered;
leading foot, trailing foot,
leading foot, trailing foot.

It was a wise instinct indeed
that made you wary
as a head would crack open
on the stair as easily
as an egg dropped on the pavement.
Humpty Dumpty's warning heeded.

But then, having let go of the railings,
progress comes quickly; doubles, then,
showing off to yourself, triples
all at speed, up or down.
Only one challenge left
to mark you as a master;

the proof test, so to speak,
the jump to the landing
from 5 or 6 steps at least
ideally from the halfway spot.
Fear before the leap and
the paratrooper's heavy landing.

Agile as a monkey at five
with the strength and reflexes
to make you an animal,
but also the monkey's 3D mind map.
Hence the hippocampus
the size of a coal bunker.

Having every drop and angle
route, nook and cranny
at instant recall
with the muscle memory
to enable evasion or expedient
depending on who's asking.

Year on year, up the stairs
to the hoose, doun the stairs
tae the back, thousands of times
not to forget 'chap door, run away'
or hide and seek
no metaphor to say it was good training.

When combined with running away
from big boys (or standing up to them)
scaling brick walls, fingering crack by crack,
vaulting fences, negotiating barbed wire
made you by nine a miniature commando
virtually any obstacle could be overcome.

Looking back over fifty years
it's easy to see this
as a preparation for a life
that doesn't exist anymore
gone like the washhouse, leeries
and outside toilet.

What need in this hi-tech electronic
virtual game playing world
for people who know how to
defy the stairwell
by climbing *outside* the railings
all the way to the top landing?

But something of this other world
still runs in the blood
the forever physical presence of the commando
albeit in wee boy form
that still resonates when you close the door
and walk over to the boss's desk.

for Dougie, remembering his visit to the project manager.

EASTERHOOSE

We lived there once
for a short while.
Farmed out
in desperate family circumstances
to relatives that were,
how to say,
not so keen for our ward-ship

coming as it did
without stipend
and anyway worn out
with wee sma hours balling
of **hoors, hairies and drunks**
constant **midgie fires**
and **stabbings.**

Even the most intrepid of voyages
begins innocently enough.
Ours began at an ordinary
bus stop outside
the subway station.
Two wee boys, heavy bags
and heavier hearts.

Ah, there it is, Number 41.
Mind and check, mum said.
*Excuse me, does this bus
go to Easterhouse?*

That depends…, said the conductor,
on how brave the driver is feeling.
Glasgow humour? Maybe not!

Travelling through familiar
home territory
we noticed ordinary citizens
seemed to shun the service
even though
it was on their route.
Afraid?

that perhaps some bampots
who were going 'aa the wey',
in both senses, would start
with 'bad language' before ending
with the rhetorical, *Whit ur*
you lookin at?; where every
answer is wrong! At last,

the press of tenements gave way
to the open spaces of Barlanock.
And, as we left the city limits,
the bus sped ever faster
as if a stagecoach
racing over the badlands
before the ambush.

To us tenement rats
the flat open landscape
was a wonder. It really seemed
that we were on a journey
to another land.
And then we saw the sign.
Ten feet tall on the gable end.

Standing nearby, presumably,
the welcoming party of natives.
A shilpit, peely-wally version
the likes of which Stanley
might have passed exploring
the Congo gesticulating fiercely
and waving **axes,** clubs and yes,

…..a **samurai sword**!
The welcome sign?
Grim irony and a trick.
The driver,
an Easterhouse route veteran,
knew the score.
Welly to the floor,

we screamed by at 55mph.
Duck, duck!,
the conductor shouted
as a flurry of **missiles**
slammed home harmlessly
although not to the nerves
judging by the **screams.**

Our destination; Lochend Road.
The end of the line
in every sense imaginable.
Standing in the apocalyptic landscape
of **broken bottles, dug shite
and burnt bin contents**
that was the circus garden feature

we realised without
knowing the words
that we had exchanged
one purgatory for another.
To be said in its favour,
there was nothing
hidden about the place,

its true nature was revealed
in a glance:
Broken, cheap, ruled
(if that is the right word)

by **knife** packing idiots.
What you see is what you get.
Steak knife? *Want some?*

It was not meant to be so.
Plans had been drawn up
by the City Fathers
who knew best
what the people needed
fresh air-*Aye, ha ha!,*
between them and us.

Okay, seriously now
get the smoke out of their lungs
a reasonable ambition
in that coal powered world
of reeking lums and hacking coughs,
but all other 'thinking'
was deficient..

Let us be conscious, Gentlemen,
of keeping costs down.
(except for the backhanders).
Budget stuff, then. Done quickly
the great unwashed-literally-
went to their new homes
with baths,

but not shops, pubs, clubs,
jobs, busy corners, parks,
streets on which one could have
a merry meeting, quiet stroll
or window shop accordingly.
Transport? Okay, No 41 service.
But not too often;

We don't want these toe-rags
coming back too soon.
Why do you think we put them there?
And that decent majority living
in falling down tenements
in Brigton, Shettleston
or Cowcaddens betrayed

by a fantasy view of the world
shared by the council heid yins
who, heady with the puffed up talk
of these idealistic days,
were thinking big. They'd put
Glasgow back on the map.
They got that right!

The knives clattering into bins
made wonderful photos
for the rest of the world
but, really, what **chibman**

worth his salt tosses away
a perfectly good **bayonet**,
even if Frankie Vaughan asks?

We looked out of our auntie's window
at this Brave New World
created by the joint mind-power
of louts and council Stalins.
A world of fresh air and baths
to be sure
and total freedom

to vandalise and terrorise.
A paradise for **hooligans,
fire-raisers and wee tollies.**
Ay ready to join in with
the kicking once, we noted,
the victim was grounded.
Take that, ya baster!...

We were given the option
of going to school
or not as we chose
some choice when the kids
in the back, our future schoolmates,
were playing at **setting fire to bins**
by setting fire to bins.

They're not that bad really,
our aunt explained.
Yous can go to the school thegether.
Can we really no go tae school
if we don't want tae?
Aye, I mean, naw!
I've got tidying up to get on wi.

So school it was then.
And after the first day offers
of **Square-goes**, either
accepted (Jim) or rejected (me)
life took on the air of normality
that it always does
given a little time

and while
we never got used to the
crash of the stairwell
the **airgun pellet's zzzip**
or our auntie having
a conversation with a neighbour
through the wall

fire engines attending
burning sofas scarcely merited
a second glance.
In bed, the late-night revellers,

screaming harlots, the **crash**
of glass and police sirens
became background noise.

Like the owl's hoot to a country dweller.

The bus ride too lost
much of its excitement when
the corporation assigned conductors
who could, as the saying goes,
'handle themselves'
and the police provided escort cars
with the **Heavy Eight** at the weekend.

They say that time can make a sofa
out of the hardest bench.
We never stayed long enough to find out
if this applied to Easterhouse.
First impressions still ran strong
that final day we took our bus
oot and hame.

Prisoners released from mistaken incarceration.
Too relieved to be happy.

Much now has changed to see
from the wild days
when 'Welcome to Rebel Land'

greeted the visitor vigilant
for a Glasgow style of calling card
a **brick** coming through
the bus window.

The feral lawns
of head-high grass have gone
and with them, I suppose,
the tigers or Japanese soldiers
that allegedly lived in them.
Big guns no longer talk
when the ice-cream van comes calling.

The patient was bled
of citizens, replaced with CCTV.
It's an improvement that's a fraction
of our hopes and desires,
but an improvement;
in a special Glasgow sense
of improvement.

Looking back I see that
time has not softened
the hard edges of that experience
or found some new
character building significance
to the threat of a
chibbing.

and left as a legacy
a conditioned response
to Yankee Doodle
that sets the teeth on edge.

Inheritance

It was a life not given to accumulation
rightly you placed no value
on things that served no purpose
in the domestic routine.

Hence the absence of a display cabinet
with its never used tea services,
EPNS cruets, China figurines,
cut lead crystal jugs.
Money could be better spent
on mince and coal.

Your wedding handsel was
a claes basket wi line and pegs
ever practical things
not viewed as a symbol
of female oppression,
but as what they are.

Part time in the dairy at 12
Full time in mill at 14
in your generation
'the bread line' was
no mere figure of speech
Wash Day fully meant what it said.

When money is tight
it's best to keep things simple

cultivate frugal habits
mend and make do
find joy in life as it is lived
look after the pennies.

you found this fairly easy to do
it was how you were brought up
hard-working, practical *and* solvent
for you knew if you skipped
a payment the factor really was
the bogey man in the dunny.

But you were no Philistine
that scorned the lighter side
yours was no creed of austerity
that took pleasure in denial
nor were you judgemental
on those who were different:

Let them sort their life
as they see fit.
And Good luck to them!

It was never about money
I know your frugality
was not simply a response
to a struggle to make ends meet,
but an expression of the simplicity
of your character.

I see it now that you were
a philosopher of sorts;
the best sort.
Unthinking in your wisdom
conclusions reached by
the genius of your race.

A wisdom that ran
down the hard centuries
to taproots in that ancient land.
With this pedigree in the bones
what need of words
to say a keenly felt truth.

Find value in your own life
as it is lived for others
and in love and duty served
find a happiness
that needs no distractions.
...*as if you had the time!*

Now I understand you
were a traveller in your own life
who packed light
the better to cover the ground
and witness the view
unencumbered.

And so, in your going
you left as little
as a bushman
of things for the loft,
but understanding the true value
of gear worth gaitherin

left me an inheritance
I would not swap
for the world.

Right here, right now
I sense you sitting next to me
sharing the wee stool
and a cup of tea
in front of the fire
quiet, content, complete, forever.

The deceased's flat

The door swung open and the smell rushed out
like a foul thing breathing in your face
in reflex I turn my face aside
BO, dust, fermenting socks, never washed nylon shirts
worse than a zoo.
Something died here before the deceased.

A house, not so much a home,
as a lair from which to make forays
to the pub and bookies
every room a skip; like a dirty form of installation art
titled *Contempt for Housekeeping*. Inexplicable;
down feathers everywhere, even on the kitchen worktop.

Furniture, the grease polished by arse and cuff.
A collection of 80s budget TVs, all broken
(your TV throwing days long gone).
Bedclothes you would not want to touch without gloves.
Not a thing worth having; a toe-rags bequest.
Our inheritance-a terrible warning: Keep to the tea!

Then I see him for the first time in a dozen years
tossed down on the 'coffee table', a bus pass
adjectives rush around to explain the carbuncular face
baboon's arse? easily a gargoyle
already looking like a cadaver
bevvy merchant's nose, red and puffy like a gland.

Shocked by his appearance I consider his life
as represented by what I see and know
floor littered with hundreds of bookie's slips.
You still evidently believed in your trebles and multipliers,
the source of the family's hope and despair,
but hit instead a lifetime losing streak.

And yet you bucked the system
living the life you wanted
staying true to your instinct for bevvy and bookies
of course, you loved your family
if love is just a word.
We both know this flat is evidence of a happy life. Yours.

'It happened quickly', the policeman said kindly.
You came home reeling
but this time different
it was not just the drink
this bell sounding really was
the last order.

Jaiket tossed aside, ready still for the square go
you staggered to the bed
with the final goodnight punch
did you regret, at that moment when the light dimmed,
the same that you dished out in your younger
more dapper, more quick-fisted days?

And so:
It all came together in the end;
the fags, the bevvy, the squalor,
a life lived in front of the TV
and bitter at the bar counter
in an equation that ends in something less than zero.

His was a rags to rags to rags story
a selfish, angry, poor wee boy that grew up
to become a bigger version of the same
the darker, meaner, Glasgow version
of Peter Pan.
My Da. RIP.

King Rab's Land
(Kinning Park, 1970)

In six feet letters, KING RAB ROOLS,
proclaiming ownership of all
his eye surveys
in the midgie and up his close.
He was more a kind of sub king really
even to his wee sisters
and MacLean Street was no Tara.

Just before they binned the place
I went back with my Instamatic
and a youth's new-found enthusiasm
for photography.
A Glasgow Ansel Adams recording
the last days of a vanishing
in the old empire's second city.

Demolishers had just started
leaving ragged tenement stumps
interspersed with piles of rubble
and scraped flat ground
creating the gap-toothed effect
(this being Glasgow)
of a brick smacked on the mouth.

Behind defiant curtains a few
stalwarts held out, too choosy
for Pollok or Nitshill.

Imagine, the cheek o them. Fancyin
themsels a cut above the lave!
It was they who kept the fire-raisers
at bay.

Broken windows apart and
the occasional sliced through
bedroom complete with pictures
still on the wall three floors up
it looked the same,
but it felt so different with
the background hum

and bang of industry and
the cries of playing children
gone forever
this time, forever really meant it.
Kinning Park was reduced to a street plan
in this silent and vacant place
the mind kept asking,

Where is everyone?
Although I knew the answer
which, although still quite
wet plaster fresh paint new,
was already ugly with implication
of a future that would be
worse than the past.

Dereliction always seemed
so eloquent in other people's world,
but not here.
The artist in me defeated.
Who wants pictures of falling down slums
and scruffy empty streets
and rat ridden back courts?

Emptied of people it became a nothing
sort of place
no more interesting than a pile
of dirty bedclothes which just happened
to be sitting on the pavement
near my old close.
I declined the photo opportunity.

Three blackened-faced teenage
lead hunters from Govan
(you could tell) emerged
from behind a bent back sheet of
corrugated metal that had been
blocking off a close mouth
instinctively bypassing curiosity and suspicion

they eyed me and my camera
with unconcealed hostility;
three to one with something worth stealing,
this is what they were reared for.

I knew the plot well enough
to know it was time to go.
And quickly!

And so, I missed the chance to have
a record of the midden
where Dunky ate the biscuits
straight off the ashes
The wash hoose where all kinds
of secret deals and viewings took place
7-0 (no idea what it refers to) FTQ

MENTOL TEAM. FTP 1690, KP STAR
YA BASS, the pends dunnies crumbling lums
snakes and ladders geography
of the closes, stairs and backs,
still strongly enough known today
that they still couldn't catch me.
And of ,course, KRR; King Rab Rools.

Of how so very Scottish that place was
in a small shades of grey way.
Hard used and broken but yet
properly viewed (and I don't
mean drunk!) it had a certain
something worth keeping.
Alas!, beyond the range of words

and known only to us
it was a better place than
its looks suggested,
an honesty about its person
a rough humour to go
with the roughness. Is this
what is meant by community?

....

Things haven't went so well
for the king since he was forced
from his kingdom
for the rebel lands of the Drum.
Firstly, he's just plain Rab now
married a witch queen, now divorced
problems naturally wi the bevvy

and his joints and the Social
scarcely rools his own house,
but still commands the kettle and afternoon TV
both of which he put on
and looked out of the window
at gang of shell-suited-junkie-dealer types
at the corner texting

Rab turned quickly in case
they saw him looking
he'd have a wee cup of tea and a slice of toast

before going to collect his grand-daughter
from school if he stepped on it
he'd have time to nip into the bookies,
he was due a bit of luck.

Homeland

Generalities

Kinning Park was not as lovely
as it sounds to ignorant ears.
The park part long turned to squares
of dirt and ashes.
In character, a bit of a battered
buffer zone between Govan
and Gorbals, best thought of
as Prodonia
and the Catholic Free State, respectively.

And sharing some of the hostile pop
as it kept these troublesome neighbours apart.
Rough enough if you're looking for trouble.
Quiet enough if you're not;
Friday nights, Old Firm days and the occasional
recreational razor fight between gangs excepted.

Specifics

Somewhere in the Indian Ocean
about 1922: The Chief being detained,
Alec, as the Second, invited
in his place to dine with some posh
(literally, in this case) English
en route for a marriage and a tiger shoot.

Alec, feeling a wee bit inferior
in those class-conscious days
watched his ps and qs carefully and
enjoyed a well-earned compliment
on his accent as a result.

This unmanned him when asked
where he came from,
Kinning Park, he said truthfully.
Oh, that sounds quite lovely, someone remarked
and faced with these confident vowels,
but now afraid of a truth, he instantly judged
would make him seem like a toe-rag from
the Glasgow slums,
Alec, gauging it safe at 6000 miles range,
to play the Judas without fear of exposure
said, *Oh, yes, lots of trees, quite nice really.*

Hoping this would kill the topic.
Which, of course, when you want it to,
it never does.
And he was obliged to continue
in his fictional description
until the enquirer was satisfied
with the charming little village
described. Possibly even thinking
of visiting it someday.

Lunch over and Alec having
his valves and dials to check
took his leave when a toff
stopped him in his tracks,
his eyes playful,

*I suppose Kinning Park must have changed a bit since
I was last there. You don't find many trees on McLellan
Street, as I recall.*

Riveted to the deck plates
Alec's look of surprise
was hardly less than if he
had been suddenly slapped
and following it a wave of shame
rushed through shrivelling everything
in its passing

caught like a schoolboy and
seeing his apostolic shame
all afternoon reflected
in the shiny glass faces
of his pressure dials
decided to pass this story on
to his children as a warning:
Never be a Judas
for something as cheap
as approval.

Conclusion

Knowing for a fact that if you deny
your homeland it will come
to claim its own,
even out there wherever that is.

Traitor

In a wee secret corner
behind the coal yard
through a loose but not
yet broken fence next
to the railway line
we built our world
with patience and planks

and corrugated sheets

only Prince and Sabre
the yardies saw us and
after intense inspection,
a very tense moment,
their shared glance agreed
and judged us unworthy
of even a growl and returned

prowling for bigger meat.

This place of ours
was no lean-to against
the bomb shelter wall
in the spare ground
waiting for the local
Luftwaffe to kick
it down around our heads.

No, this was the real thing, it actually kept the rain out.

and we would probably
live in it for the rest of our lives
secure contained happy
there was a candle and a bottle
of ginger to toast our genius
in creating our space in
a world busy with spies,

tell-tale girls and big boys.

Even while we pretended
we knew it could not last
eventually spotted some
informer would call down
Vandals on our secret den
our time there was marbled
by this fear of reality arriving

sudden and ugly.

I has no idea how ugly
until arriving as arranged
with a jammy piece and
some broken biscuits I entered
the hatch heart leaping with love
to find another sharing our den
by invite. By invite!

The serpent in our wee Eden.

A claw gripped my heart and
squeezed a pain beyond words
instantly morphed to monstrous
anger which directed inward consumed
my love as a hungry wolf
a dead carcass and I was left
as I still am.

Torn

to live a life as a sort of
collateral damage a clichéd
song of waiting for the
betrayal
knowing it will come but
resolving next time to take
my biscuits and ginger with me.

Wedding Dress

On ma mammy's instruction
I threw oot her wedding dress.
It had sat under the bed
for twenty years.
She didnae look at it
jist, *Here, put this auld dress
in the midden, will ye.*

I pretended not to know it
but Louise and I often played
at beautiful brides with it
whenever she was oot the hoose.

It was silk and I am sure still
worth a few bob but
she was too proud to think of
selling it and too superstitious
to pass it to me or Louise
in case some dark spell
was trapped in the lace netting.

In any case, even then
I would've ripped it too ribbons
just getting it on. She must have been
an elf on her wedding day!
It would've fitted Louise
she takes eftir Mammy
and is lighter boned than me.

It had been a symbol of the glorious
start of a journey
in hope and love, now
it was an equal symbol
almost mocking
in its dusty but dignified loveliness
of the opposite

and a reminder
that the fair following wind
can suddenly swell with anger
and ruin you
and the safe harbour,
no matter how clearly sighted,
is always an illusion
until the box is nailed.

I was twelve years old.
I already knew who I was going to marry.
My life and our children easy and loving
a walk in the sun through a garden alive
with warm and colour and birdsong.
So I thought.

I took the dress doun the stairs
and, worried some back court arab
would find it during a treasure search,
went to the fullest bin

and scraped the top contents
of ash eggshells and filth
into the box

not realising the magic of the gesture
or that fickle fates' hex sits where
it will; joyous beginnings, merry moments
and even old boxed wedding dresses
sitting on a pile of tattie peelings.

Three Fingers

Perhaps from seeing the buckle work lose
or finding it a bit scabby looking
to hold up trousers as sharp as his were,
he must have thought, *It's time now.*
The oldest having turned six.

Maybe he got the idea
in a flash of inspiration
as he raised the washing
on the pulley and hooked
the cord at shoulder height

thinking, *I know something else
that would sit over the hook.*
And be at instantly reachable height
like a gun over the fireplace
to keep down the natives
when they became lippy
or light-fingered with the biscuit tin.
or just because…

And so, the buckle removed and then
three fingers cut as if one for each child.
Why d'ye do that, Daddy?
So it's mair sore.
Soon put to the test
with, in fairness to him,
equality of application to each child
and reasonably consistent standards.

Talking, talking back, talking cheeky,
cheeky expressions, moaning,
not liking the dinner, not eating
the same with sufficient relish,
coming in late, coming in early
and especially talking in bed.
And then, greetin too much
after the leathering.

His M.O; a lightning
fighter-bomber raid on the legs
which writhed on the mattress
like pyjamad eels
under a lash which snapped
loud as firecrackers.

The children soon discovered
the three fingers to be
a borrowed idea from the classroom
which version, at full military strength,
made father's home-made job a quite benign,
even kindly, way to teach the lesson;
Shut up when telt and take
your medicine without girnin.

Lesson taught so well that lashings
of ten to the dozen were soon accepted
with the same natural equanimity
as a pat on the shoulders.

The home message reinforced at school again
and again and again right up to The Law's,
'*Time, Gentlemen, please!*' bell.
There will be no more belting of children.
From now on the children will be belting us.

They have been well prepared
and isn't that the truth.

Gorbals Triptych

Part 1: Carrying

Part 2: A Mark of Distinction

Part 3: Balancing the Equation

CARRYING

as edged weapons go
it's not much to look at.
Clear from your mind
the warrior and his claymore,
rapier, bayonet, even
the crudest cutlass
is in another league.

It shares a pedigree
in stealth with the
hieland chibman's choice,
but even the skean dhu
in comparison
is a prince to a pauper

but, unlike the bread knife,
which clattering to the floor,
strains credibility with the,
*Ma mammy gied mi it fir
cuttin ma piece* explanation
(especially if you get free dinners)

if caught, all you need is
a bit of brass neck.
Got tae keep masel lookin sharp, Sir.
Hold their gaze, they cannae
prove anything!

Finding its natural home
in sock or neatly fitted
under the tailored triple pleat
of an Arthur Black when heidie
or polisman comes hunting
enforcers of a chib ban

hidden innocuous until
that moment arrives,
as we know it must,
when it does its job,
the treacherous cut.

Ladies and Gentlemen,
Neds, Bams and Hairies;
I give you, the wee steelie
aka, the sharpened steel comb.

A MARK OF DISTINCTION

Two principles; one social, one scientific.
Each seeks distinction in their own field.
All life tends towards equilibrium.

Stevie, chess club champ excelling
in all subjects. He even got
the techie prize. FFS!
(could he no even gie the

wooden heids a wee chance?)
It could be said fairly, if
somewhat manifestly unfairly,
the school's distinction rested
every year again and again
and again on his one person;
no more reason needed then.

All we need
is the time and place
for the judgement.
Oh, and the judge!

Cue Fleckie:
In a parallel universe
he had made a name
in the field of ...plastic surgery
in a sort of anti-sense.

Fairly, his hird's achievements
rested on his person
a kind of dux
the Leader Aff.

He'd heard of this brainy cunt
at his old school
radar tracked his achievements
and understood at protozoan level

the need to resolve the equation
whose components each represented
whatever the fuck that meant.

BALANCING THE EQUATION

Matter and anti-matter fated
to meet the inevitability of
synchronicity lunch-time
coppers called away, Fleckie
and the hird hanging, borrowing
change from pies and bridies.
Steelie in tap jaiket pocket
and Stevie crossing the
school playground unaware
it was now a laboratory
testing under Gorbals parameters
something like an equation
BC (KP) +(C+3N) =
There's that big nosed brainy cunt.

Thorough and careful in his MO
(he was a nutcase not an idiot)
Fleckie scoped him.

Alone; check!
No witnesses that would dare; check!
Tooled; check!

Feeling the precision with which
he was being moved to the conclusion
he stepped into the arena,
his arena.

The neds in close attendance
on their leader blocked off Stevie
Fleckie flanked his phalanx
appearing suddenly in front
wearing a face like a hatchet.

Hey, Cuntie!
Think yir fuckin smart?
Understanding that this was
the prelude to the inevitable
conclusion playground life
stopped and arranged itself
around the periphery.

Run Stevie Run! But finding his motor
stripped of gears and his tongue lost
overwhelmed with the mathematical
certainty of the product just about
to be produced.
All he could see was a box of knives,
all he could hear was them jingling.
Ahm talkin tae yoo.
Maybe, he's too busy workin oot

a new formula?
…Well, work this oot!

Seen from the common room window
a silver flash startling in its brightness
going up the way.
No mouthed O, just bent double
like the supporting strings of
a puppet cut, a deep well opened

and Stevie's shirt turned red quickly.

Then, as night creatures suddenly caught
by the dawn, fearing exposure
and realising what they had done,
as Stevie stood there pumping
blood like slitted ox,
they cut tail and fled

underground, or wherever it is they hang out

to emerge in the near future
on a fast track to a richly deserved
rest in the big hoose.
While Stevie recovering his nerves
and nose, which now sports
a quite fetching schlager scar,

continued to collect accolades,
but with an appreciation
that success always comes
with a price and payment
will be collected eventually
in blood.

In the interests of anonymity the protagonists names have not
been changed.

Jungle Juiced

There it sat alongside
distinctly British fare
Bridie and beans, Fried
egg roll, Pie and chips,
Custard and snotter tart
promising something
exotic in the Co-op canteen.

Having no sense of the
deceit or even irony in
its name (this being
the Gorbals, after all!)
we accepted it for what
it claimed to be: juice from
the jungle; *No, really!*

Perhaps modified to fit
with Glasgow tastes;
even more sugar more
chemicals garish colours.

Asking for it suggested a
sense of foreign adventure
a drink especially appreciated
after a long day with
the machete, and actually
there may be some truth
in this last statement

for some street corner
gourmets of Ballater Street.

The colour of bile and
tasting of chemicals and gas
in an age before healthy
it was the healthy option
the bubbles helping to
dissolve the triple dose
of saturates and salt hiding

under brown sauce
before the less healthy
option of leaving the
safety of the canteen
laager for the jungle
clearing that was the
street and hostile natives

taking tribute to purchase
libations for their own
jungle juice god before
giving permission to
travel across their territory
to Brigton, Gorbals Cross
or Glasgow Green.

Cutting a Deal

Part one: cutting

the American Barber wasn't
from America and had
never been there although
he had been a bullfighter
so the poster said

and perhaps the lack
of drama since giving up
the cape to take the scissors
had led him to
take up the drink too

so that it wasn't unknown
for an angry mum
to turn up with a recently
cut child for the line
to be levelled (eventually)

under the smiles of Tony Curtis and Dean Martin

he once cut my ear
which fact I hid from
my parents as I assumed
it to be my fault.
Blood discount, no chance.

Part two: a deal

Dunky noticed wee Turnip
wearing a cowboy hat and
walking like he was carrying
money, *Where ye aff tae?*
The American fir a herrcut.
How much ye got?
Two and six.

Go haufers on the hauf croun, then?
You get 6d an I get the ither hauf,
***and** I'll cut yer hair for nothing.*
Turnip not having done money
in school yet liked the idea
of sixpence worth of sweeties.
Deal done, easy peasy.

So, Dunky sneaked out
his mum's dressmaking scissors
and in the dunny gave
wee Turnip a haircut to
remember, or maybe forget!
Dunky discovered it was
trickier than it seemed

but he persevered to keep
his side of the bargain

in the half light
it seemed passable,
but really words cannot
do justice to what sat
on wee Turnip's head

who couldn't see it, but
wouldn't have minded anyway.
His mum did!
I know he's got a drink problem,
but this is absolutely ridiculous!
Twenty minutes later Dunky
sees wee Turnip getting towed

powerfully along by his mum
heading for the show-down
with the American, whose
bullfighter skills were never
going to be more needed.
Dunky also saw in daylight
the results of his handiwork

looking something like a bird's
nest after a fire and a storm
and also that the cut on the ear
was looking much worse now.
Oh, how he wished he could

go back in time and give
wee Turnip his money back.

Too young for the Foreign Legion,
and knowing the brothers
would track him down anyway,
Dunky had no choice but to wait
(shiting himself) on the fall-out
from a deal gone bad.
But having learned the lesson

early in life that when cutting
a deal you need to think it through
all the way to the escape plan:
Full refund if the posse catch you up,
or at least bus fare put aside ready
if you see them turning the corner
before they see you.

Treasure Trove

The story of two tanners

On TV, a news item about a
find of buried treasure and
the speculation about why
no-one came back for it.

A lengthy list was proffered
but missed out one well known
to me.

****

A dream and a nightmare come true
simultaneously, for me for him
respectively.

Fist like a boulder so hard
had he held its contents
and then his hand opens
on the change, *Here, Mammy.*
which is,… **da daaa!**
(heard in my head)
.........not there!

A magician's trick certainly
but gone terribly wrong.
Three mouthed Os.

Her him me, but above my O
and behind my eyes hidden
the drug of victory coursing
round and round dizzy with delight
at her disappointment in him.

I almost jumped at the
all conquering triumph of
his failure.

The Germans have a word for this pleasure.

He had begged and cajoled
for weeks to usurp my role
as the message-getter to prove
he was a big boy as good
as any girl at nipping down
to the dairy or the fruiterer.

And too, to lever in on my stipend
of a go at the penny tray
if any change was left.
Finally he gets his chance
and I feel resentment strongly
out of proportion.

Stripped of my medal of office
I would get him back

and especially after the look
of triumph flashed to me
as he set off for the dairy with
the significant trust

of a single half crown

admittedly given to make it easy
to carry in his little fist instead
of the giant coins (this being
pre-decimal days when British coins
were strength building)
that would have made the exact amount.

Don't lose the change, mum said.

and he did. **Vindication.**

So were sent back double-quick
to search the route before
some street magpie
spots the glint and turns it to sweeties.

I was such a magpie
and spotted the two tanners
next to each other shining like two staring eyes .
The three pennies were gone.

He had dropped the change, or
more likely, laid it down when he
had climbed through the space
in the wall to cut across the back
to the close

and I had found it;
mission accomplished.
Mum would be pleased
then as I picked them up
and just before I shouted
for joy at my success,
as if a hand restrained me

and other darker options
although not yet even formed
took hold. And I let them.

Let him sweat and serves her
right for picking him over me!

Quickly snatched them up and,
to a background of my wee brer
sobbing in his search,
I pretended to look along the walls edge
where I surreptitiously scrapped a deep slot
with a stick and jammed the tanners in

rim matching rim. And covered it.
Buried treasure. It really does exist.

I'd dig the loot up later, cleverly noting
the exact spot by the markings
on the brick wall above.
It felt great.

Already sly enough at six to know
that I couldn't just rush round
to Susan's shop ten minutes later
for a double go at the threepenny tray,
like a daft boy would
if he had stolen it, knowing that she
would be suspicious of me
with a tanner and say something
that would put me on the spot,
Uncle visiting?

Or worse, sneaking off somewhere else
to still get spotted with someone thinking,
Why did she go there for her sweeties?
for it eventually to get back to mum.
As it would.

No, I'd need to sit on the loot
think about how I could access it
risk free.

The thinking took seconds, I'm sure
the devil noticing me
as a potential recruit, planted the idea
just like that. Got it;
wait until dad was drunk
(not much of a wait) and then
the next day spend it and claim,
if necessary, that he had given me it.

He would say aye, so as not to make it seem like he had forgotten.

Problem sorted, easy.
Enjoy the wicked pride
of my intelligence.
Top girl in class **and** top girl on the street
and now back home
for the second course of schadenfruede.
Life was good.

Wee brer gets a small sherricking
and a massive dose of disappointment.
He'd lost 1/3; that wasn't the nothing then
it is now.

But the second lashing
wasn't nearly so enjoyable as I'd imagined.
In fact, seeing his sad wee face
I said to mum, *It's not his fault, Mum.*

Big sis instinct forgetting for a moment
what I'd done
and she just looked at me quietly
something telling in my voice?
As if she knew.

Almost caught.

I never went back for the money.
I didn't know why then
I now know that somehow
I felt it to be the wages of sin
without knowing the phrase.

For I never forgot where it was
but the feeling of guilt was strong
and it put a hex on it
tempting me to sell my soul
for a Bunty and the sweetie trays.

The place is long gone but
the money will still be there
perhaps some future age
metal detectorist will find it and
know that the coins could not
have just been dropped like that
and wonder why the burier
never returned; listing

the common sense reasons
but missing one. The true one;

sometimes you don't want to.

Growing up With the Brigade

Calling the companies to order
purpose mounts in the cold damp air
with the paradiddles tinny pulse
it feels like duty demanding its place

same feeling the night before as we Brasso buckle Blanco
cartridge belt shine the cap number thoughtfully made removable

Then the bagpipes lift off
ripping the air apart as we
wheel left in orderly columns
disciplined and 20,000 strong

for that purpose. 30 Company, Kinning Park's finest better than
the 101 or the Govan lads our elite little band decent wee boys

a show of strength Empire style
to some dignitary visiting the toun
pedestalled with the provost nodding
as we troop past and salute, *Ey…ees, left!*

led by decent men instilled with the same duty and purpose.
We'd have won the war in '42 wi lads like yous!

Afterwards back at the assembly point
our marching demeanour boots and
accoutrements were favourably compared
with any and every other company

once were told when on parade although admittedly by an
auld jakey who I now see saw the truth of us quite clearly despite.

Praised prayered and dismissed
formally then a, *Well done, Lads,*
I'm proud of you. We left for bag of chips
and the subway home.

Moving forward but unknowingly already in the past marching in step
but out of step with the age of television and technology

The whole day stretching out in front
in which we could do anything as
we had already done something big
none of us had let the side down

but actually waiting on the anomie of the internet
to take us to a new anarchy beyond the realm of imagination.

and we understood what that meant.
Now that is a legacy to stand beside
knowing how to wheel, salute, stand
to attention and march in step silently.

wee brer

Admittedly having the toughest
dad in the world boosts confidence
but he was not there that day
when you, as they now say,
'seized the moment' and crossed
the road to the hird-less bully

to test alone his mettle against
his swagger, sneer and threats
your heart as hard as the granite
cobbles you walked over
an Achilles in shorts
(actually my old ones)

with holes in your shoes
stuffed with cardboard.
Mum said, *Where are you going?*
Jist tae see some'dy.
I knew when I saw clenched fists
what this was about and

my stomach hosed in acid like
it would burn through to my shirt.
Were the gang around the corner?
Not much was said I think
Dae ye want tae try noo?
I saw him hesitate and his

unexpected supplicant gestures
Dad always said to hit first
keep on going until it's over
you lamped him he went down
like you'd hit him with a hauf brick
it's over.

Bursting proud of you
I nearly stopping passers-by
That's ma wee brer, there!
Mum was shocked. When
she told Dad that you'd given
him a full 3d worth and no change

perhaps it was the only time
he was really proud of you
coming back later from the pub
with the champion's portion
a bottle of lemonade
and a bag of crisps.

Time goes by Jim went to London
and became a James a polished
version of himself the world
went cork-popping right and
then as it inevitably does
went all wrong.

Fortune's smile having beguiled
turns aside to some other fool
and urbane James becomes
plain old Jim once again
with holes in his shoes again, and
no future worthy of its name.

Perhaps Jim, the soft London
water has washed clean
your memory although
White Flash won't have helped
and so I'm the only witness
to Mum's astonished face

Dad's pride and the resolve
you once had that is yet
still hard enough to smash
through the barriers
of ill-use and ill-fortune
which surround your life.

Hard enough to take you
over the road once again
to something that needs
taught a lesson.

Also Available

Love's Troublesome Journey

Is it love, need it always be trouble and how can it be a journey if you end up back where you started without having left? Oh, and how come he knows so much about love? All this is made clear in this collection.

Central to the human experience and always losing

The Belt Room

A cross my heart true collection about some more than average tough schools in Glasgow during the '60's and '70's. It especially considers the use of corporal punishment (the belt) as a standard pedagogic technique; the author is well qualified to comment.

The final record of that double belted generation who are now on life's home run.

Visit www.glenntelfer.me